LIVE A LITTLE, LOVE A LOT

A collection of poetry by Elaine Gibbons

LIVE A LITTLE, LOVE A LOT

Published by A Poem On The Wall.com

978-0-9930558-0-5

Photograph, cover design and editing by Damian Hull.

ACKNOWLEDGEMENT

I acknowledge my debt to God, and thank him for this wonderful gift.

SPECIAL THANKS
To my mom, brothers and sisters, who have always loved and encouraged me. Damian my computer technician, he never fails to put my ideas into practice. To Bruce Johnson who has encouraged me from day one. Mr Handsworth MBE you gave me an opportunity to shine, and a platform from which to elevate. My brother in law Errol Fraser, thank you for the kind words. To Paul who has supported me over many years.

EXTRA SPECIAL THANKS TO;
My sister Kathy Fraser, for being my proof-reader and for encouraging me to do more. My niece Rae who has always been there when I've needed a favour. Bentley Noble who has inspired me and been a constant source of support, in all that I have done. To my children Stacey and Simeon, I love you and am proud of you both. Grandson Malachi, you will always be my little soldier.

A special message to all who have read and supported my work, Thank You so much be blessed.

This book has been written in memory of my father, Mr Rodan Gibbons. R.I.P dad, your memory lives on.

CONTENTS

From the dream to reality
The youth of today
You and me
Growing pains
Live your life
My mother
Just looking back 2013

CHAPTER 3 – its Gospel

I've been saved
His grace and mercy
He who has been good to me
My lifelong journey
I'm blessed

CHAPTER 4 – Love

Real love
Why I love you
Be mine
We all want to be loved
This was us
It's free
Simply the best
I promise

CHAPTER 5 – Memories

Saying good-bye to my dad
My neighbour my friend
In loving memory
Not forgotten
Missing you
Two years later
Rest in peace
Saying good-bye to you
Thinking of you
It was time
Fond memories
Someone so special
A dear friend

CHAPTER ONE- INSPIRATION

"Ask for what you want and expect to get it."
Maya Angelou

DREAMS

It's a small seed planted in your mind
Of something you want to do
It's a wish a wonder or ambition
It's a dream that can come true.

It's something for you to hold onto
That no-one can take away
Something you hope to live to see
As you live your lives each day.

It's something that means the world to you
You may need to work hard to succeed
You may need to keep your eye on the prize
And you may need to take the lead.

Dreams give us hope of something special
So let no-one take it away
Let no-one say your dream can't come true
Just stay focused and believe it will happen some day.

Written by Elaine Gibbons ©

DON'T GIVE UP

I know it's hard in these times we're living in
No money, no job, no hope
No prospects for your future
You don't know how your gonna cope.

It can be hard for the youth
The way the systems been set up
But they don't all have to fail,
They have to be positive, focused and be that blazing
trail.

Doors may shut and people may say no
But that ain't the end of your road
So dust yourself off and get on your feet
And get back in that mode.

Everyone's in fear of losing something
So no-one wants to give
It's no longer about the colour of your skin
But due to the times were living in.

The world's in a recession
But stay positive, focused, stand strong
If you have a vision you can live your dream
But don't let society drag you along.

It's all about your mindset
Take time to think things through
Always try and do the right thing
And you'll be blessed, I promise you.

It won't always be easy
But you just need to endure
You need to find that strength within
And see what life has in store.

Written by Elaine Gibbons. ©

TODAY

I woke up with a spring in my step
I woke up with peace in my heart
I woke up with a smile on my face
I woke up with a positive start.

Today I'll smile and say hello
To friends and strangers too
I'll try to help those that are in need
And be the best in all I do.

I'll spare a thought to those without
And give what I can give
I'll do this with a willing heart
Because that's the right way to live.

My parents taught me that kindness costs nothing
And blessings will come from above
I was taught to do my best for others
And to do it out of love.

Do good and good will follow you
Is what mother always say's
I believe this to be true indeed
So that's what I try and do always.

Don't worry about what others say
Live your life but live it the right way.

Written by Elaine Gibbons. ©

YOU ARE WHAT YOU SAY YOU ARE

I can be who I want to be
I just have to believe
I can achieve all I put my mind to
I just have to believe.

I can do that job, I can buy that house
I just have to believe
I can overcome this illness
I just have to believe.

I can pass my exams
I just have to believe
I'll be given another chance
I just have to believe.

I can be a good parent
I just have to believe
I can be that role model
I just have to believe.

I can do all things
If I only believe
In myself at all times
Great things, will I achieve.

Written by Elaine Gibbons. ©

IT'S ALL YOURS

The secret of success is you
But your attitude's got to be right
You've got to have faith and focus
It's not about to happen over night.

The secret of success is you
It's about believing in you all the time
It's about talking life into any situation
It's about telling yourself you'll be fine.

The secret of success is you
It's about not giving up on your dream
It's about not giving up at the first obstacle
No matter how hard things may seem.

The secret of success is you
Your time, your work, your gain
Your dream can manifest itself
Even under stress and strain.

The secret of success is you
You have the ability to see things through
You have the strength to know you'll make it
Even when others aren't sure of you.

A good mind, a good heart
Is the secret of your success
A positive attitude is a must
That's been the secret of my success, and in God I've
put my trust.

Written by Elaine Gibbons. ©

HAVE A LITTLE FAITH

I thought I was weak
But now know that I'm strong
I thought I couldn't achieve
But I've proved myself wrong.

I've achieved so much
Now that I've changed my mind
From negative to positive
My eyes are open, I'm no longer blind.

I'm talented and intelligent
I'm gifted and I'm smart
I can do all things if I want to
If I only do it from my heart.

If I can keep my mind clear
My dreams will remain in sight
They will become reality
And I will prove myself right.

I can now look to the future
As I know I will achieve
My goals and aspirations
This I always will believe.

So believe in yourself
As I believe in you
And know that you can do all things
That you put your mind to.

Written by Elaine Gibbons. ©

YOUNG PEOPLE

Young people of today
What is this gang culture?
Do you really believe in the cause?
Or is the effect the deciding factor?

Is it that you don't feel you belong?
Or have you got a personal issue?
When you don't come home at night
Don't you think anyone will miss you?

Young people of today
Too many of you are dying
You need to educate yourselves
And stop your parents from crying.

Young people of today
I know you want a chance in life
But you've got to change the way you think
And walk away from all that strife.

Young people of today
You need your own identity
You need to stop the bad behaviour
So you can choose your destiny.

Young people of today
You can choose weather to live or die
There need not be more casualties
You can make a difference if you try.

Young people of today
We need you as leaders and motivators
Standing up for what is right
And not as bad news, in tomorrow's newspapers.

Written by Elaine Gibbons. ©

THIS IS ME

Tell yourself that you're beautiful
Tell yourself that you're strong
Tell yourself you'll stay positive
Even, when things go wrong.

Tell yourself you'll be happy
Even when things don't go your way
When your children play up
Or your partner goes astray.

Tell yourself you'll keep smiling
Even when you want to get mad
Just tell yourself to rise above it
And don't let your loved one's see you sad.

There are many today who have nothing
No family, no job, no home
Many of us have this and more
And we still find time to moan.

Tell yourself that you're blessed
As you've lived to see another day
You've got love all around
For that I hope and pray.

Tell yourself you're loving
And worth your weight in gold
You already know you're amazing
If the total truth be told.

Written by Elaine Gibbons. ©

CHAPTER TWO-REAL LIFE

"Nothing will work unless you do."
Maya Angelou

WHATS UP BLOOD?

I hear you carry a gun
So what's that all about?
I hear you in a gang
Don't even try and shout.

Don't tell me their your family
And that their looking out for you
Because when push comes to shove
Your prison sentence they won't do.

I hear you carry a gun
So where's the fun in that
So you think you're a big man now
And it's got you pocket fat.

How can you get my respect blood?
When you carry a gun
It's the easy way out
Your just a coward my son.

You can do so much more son
Your life don't have to be this way
Just change your mind and do right
While God's blessed you with another day.

You're strong, intelligent and talented
So don't let no-one tell you, you can't
Live a life that is rewarding
Or that it's much too late to start.

Be courageous, be creative, be confident
Be the role model of today
Achieve your goals and live your dreams
But first, please put the gun away.

Written by Elaine Gibbons. ©

A DEVIL IN DISGUISE

I thought he was my angel
He was my wish upon a star
He treated me like no other
He was the best partner I'd had so far.

I fell in love and trusted him
I believed I had his heart
The first year and a half was wonderful
I didn't think we'd ever part.

He asked me to marry him
And I course I told him yes
We started planning the wedding
I even looked around for my dress.

I didn't say he was perfect
So he would, slip up once or twice
But then it became more often
It became apparent he was just telling lies.

We talked we reasoned
And he said he'd try
He slowly killed the trust I had
And then the love began to die.

It all seemed so perfect
Like every woman's dream
He'd do anything for me
He treated me like a queen.

How could something so special go so wrong?
He was a devil in disguise
When I think of how it went wrong
It was due to his lies, and more lies.

Words can't explain my feelings
Of hurt, disgust and pain
My heart now bare the scars
From falling in love again.

Written by Elaine Gibbons. ©

BACK TO LIFE

Thank you Mr Spicy
For inspiring me
Now that I've picked up my pen
I can feel who I should be.

I got lots to say
Because I feel so much
I got lots to give
I've been blessed by God's touch.

I got lots to say
And lots to imagine
I want to stop his pain
And I want to stop her crying.

I got lots to say
And I want to be a blessing
I want to encourage somebody
And I want to feel that there laughing.

I got so much to say
And I just need to pass it on
Because life's worth living
I just want to lyric you all day long.

I can feel who I should be
Now that I've picked up my pen
I need to be someone's inspiration
So I thank Mr Spicy, again and again.

Written by Elaine Gibbons. ©

MOM DON'T WORRY

Do not despair if I go off the rails
You probably did your very best
You can only grow me up so far
And then I have to do the rest.

Do not despair if I don't pass all my exams
I'm sure you encouraged me to revise
I'm old enough to make my own choice
And to live my very own life.

Do not despair if I have children early
You can only teach me what you know
I expect you were a good example
And showed me the right way to go.

Do not despair if I don't live your dreams
I am bound to have my own
Now that I have come of age
And left the family home.

Just let me grow up
And make my own mistakes
But be there with open arms
When I need comfort, from heartaches.

I am a child of the future
So try not to despair
If I don't live up to your expectations
Always let me know you still care.

Please be proud of my accomplishments
And who I have become
And that no matter what happens in my life
You'll be there to say well done.

So mothers do not despair or worry
Just try to do your very best
Teach children about love and respect
And then let them do the rest.

Written by Elaine Gibbons. ©

FATHER AND SON

Dads, what a job you have today
Some of your son's have no mind of their own
Their turning to their friends for support
He won't admit it, but he feels alone.

A son needs his father
But he refuses now to beg
For his time or commitment
So he chooses his friends instead.

A son needs his father
To teach him how to be a man
To show him different aspects of life
And to make him understand.

That as a father he has a role to play
And it's a very important part
And no matter what the circumstance
He needs to be there from the start.

Just show him that you love him
By spending quality time together
Get to know your son
So you can grow him up much better.

Your son needs his father more than his friends, the
gangs or society
He needs to know the true meaning of life
He needs to know what's false, and what's reality

It's not all about the money
It's not all about the stuff
It's about holding his head up high
When tings and times get rough.

Written by Elaine Gibbons. ©

LIVE, LAUGH AND LOVE

Live to Dream, and live your purpose
There's so much more to life than this.
No man can chose your destiny
You can live a life of bliss.

Learn to laugh at yourself
Because life's already serious enough
And even when laughing with others
Try forgetting about your baggage and stuff.

If you haven't loved, you haven't lived
So love yourself and others to
It's the greatest gift of all
And not really that hard to do.

Living, laughing and loving
This is what we're here to do
This is the source of survival
And I'm wishing It all for you.

Written by Elaine Gibbons. ©

ALL THE SINGLE LADIES

Don't go looking
Ladies let them find you
Let them give a little chase
And do what they need to.

Let them take you to lunch
Or even cook you a little dinner
Don't invite them home too early
Or give up the cherry either.

If he's interested he will wait
For he knows he's found a good thing
Accept his flowers, compliments and gift's
And hope the romance will be motivating.

Ladies praise him for his efforts
And let him know that he's the man
Let him know that he's appreciated
And do your best for him when you can.

Ladies let your man wine and dine you
Don't let your standards fall
Don't be fooled by charming words
And don't be his midnight call.

A good man loves a good woman
One with beauty and her own mind
Not one that chases rings and things
But that one of a special kind.

A woman of virtue
With independence on her side
A woman he can be proud of
And one he can call his bride.

So ladies don't go looking
For you are grand by design
Just do what you do best
And let destiny chose your time.

"He that findeth a woman, findeth a good thing"

Written by Elaine Gibbons. ©

THE PAST

I don't want to cry anymore
I don't want to live in the past
I want to forget all those years
When I believed my happiness wouldn't last.

I'm sick of feeling down and out
And feeling lost all the time
Scratching around for good fortune
And holding out for that last dime.

It's time I made my own fortune
And live my own dreams
I don't want to live in the past
My life doesn't have to be as it seems.

I can rise above this recession
I can make my feelings known
I just won't live this way anymore
I can make it on my own.

I'm gonna be positive and hopeful
I'm not gonna cry anymore
I'm gonna believe in myself
Of this I'm very sure.

It's not all about the money
It's about surrounding myself with love
I'm looking to my future
I've got the courage to rise above.

And rise above it I will
As I know my futures bright
I can now go to sleep
Without crying at night.

Written by Elaine Gibbons. ©

YOU CAN HEAL

You can learn to live without him
You can live without her too
It may not seem like that right now
But believe me you do.

Times a great healer
Is what many people say
When your hearts been broken
Or a loved one goes away.

Most people cry
While others fill the gap
With substances or others
Please, don't fall for that crap.

Talk to other people
Make your feelings known
Your not the first, nor will be the last
You don't have to be alone.

Times a great healer
It will help to mend the pain
It will give you strength to go on
So you have the chance to love again.

Written by Elaine Gibbons. ©

IT'S JUST ME

I've made the bed
And cleaned the whole place
But each time I look in the mirror
I only see my own face.

I come home from work
And sit in the same chair
One plate, one glass
Because there's no one else there.

I read a book
Or chat on the phone
But when I hang up
I'm still on my own.

I go for a drive
Or hang out with a friend
Just so another evening
On my own I don't spend.

I wake up and give thanks
I'm just happy to be alive
Sometimes it's hard being alone
But I'll certainly survive.

This is just me, an independent woman hoping to fall
in love.

Written by Elaine Gibbons. ©

I WILL

I'm taking a leap of faith
And I'm hanging on for dear life
Because I believe that one day
I will become a wife.

I will become a soul mate
And all someone will need
I will become their other half
And together we'll succeed.

We'll have challenges and trials
But we'll see them all through
We'll go from strength to strength
I'll do my best, I promise you.

I will put my faith in God
And he'll never let me go
He holds my future in his hands
And I know he loves me so.

So, so much
And more than words can say
Help me take that leap of faith
And help me as I pray.

I pray for patience
Strength and courage too
I'll put my trust in Jesus
Because he knows just what to do.

Written by Elaine Gibbons. ©

IF ONLY.......

I made so many mistakes
I wouldn't listen to reason
I never thought it would happen
But here I sit in this prison.

These four walls are not my own
But are home for the next 2 years
I had my Freedom, but now it's gone
I'm holding back the tears.

The bars are the chains that hold me
I have a number but not a name
No freedom, no friends just in-mates
To the officers were all the same.

Yes sir, no sir
I have no place outside
But from behind these walls
The rules I must abide

Some say you never know what you got till it's gone
That is the truth for me
My home, my kids my environment
That's the only place I want to be.

Time to rise, time to eat
Two hours outside and then it's time to sleep.

This cell, this wing
This ain't no life for me
But only I can make that change
If it's free I want to be.

A life of crime, is no life at all
But now I'm out, I'm gonna make that call.

A call to all who will listen
To the message I want to send
There's nothing better than Freedom
So let your life of crime, now end.

Written by Elaine Gibbons. ©
Inspired by Bentley Noble.

FROM THE DREAM, TO REALITY

He was running the streets
With his guns and drugs
He was chasing the money
Along with the other thugs.

He thought he was invincible
He was living a life of crime
Until he was sent to prison
And told he would have to do hard time.

His friends wouldn't visit
His family cared no more
His freedom was taken away
He thought he was above the law.

Prison wasn't easy
He had to do as he was told
No-where to run, no-where to hide
As his dignity began to unfold.

His 8 by 6 cell
And just a hour a day outdoors
This was the price he had to pay
He didn't know it at the time of cause.

He felt caged like an animal
Told when and where to go
When and where to sleep
He'd never ever felt so low.

He was held captive
But just wanted to be free
He was just another prisoner
But without faith, he could not see.

See, how he could change his life
From one full of sin and shame
To having joy and peace
Without laying guilt and blame.

He accepted Christ Jesus
And turned his life around
God almighty can do all things
Only through him can peace be found.

Written by Elaine Gibbons. ©
Inspired by Bentley Noble.

THE YOUTH OF TODAY

They have so many opportunities
The world is at their feet
They can be anything they aspire to be
But some don't even see it.

School's colleges and university
Diplomas, degrees and more
It takes hard work and determination
It's what some are working for.

A great job, a great career
A good example to be set
They need to be encouraged
So the important things they don't forget.

They need to have a good attitude
They need to be the very best
Only the fittest will survive
They need not worry about the rest.

Life is what you make it
You have to work hard to achieve
The world owes you nothing
But in yourself you must believe.

It's not all about the grades though
Some get a lucky break
But you have to put yourself forward
If only, for you futures sake.

Written by Elaine Gibbons. ©

YOU AND ME

Who am I?
I'm beautiful, independent and strong
Who am I?
I'm confident, but will admit when I'm wrong.

Who am I?
I'm the friend that will always be there
Who am I?
I'm the stranger, who shows that I care.

Who am I?
I'm the neighbour that gives a helping hand
Who am I?
I'm that person that tries to understand.

So who am I?
Who am I indeed?
I'm a woman of virtue
So come follow my lead.

Written By Elaine Gibbons. ©

GROWING PAINS

It's hard growing up
And being mis-understood
And told not to do, all the things
Your mind tells you, you should.

Your hair and body changes
Your hormones and attitude too
You're trying to keep up with the latest trend
But your parents can't keep up with you.

You want to branch out
And you want your freedom
You say your parents don't listen
So you threaten to leave them.

We were all young once
And know that times do change
We know your thoughts will differ
But don't let your focus go out of range.

There's nothing wrong with being different
We don't all need to be the same
You just have to remember
That life is not a game.

One heart, one mind, one life so live it.

Written by Elaine Gibbons. ©

LIVE YOUR LIFE

Some people hit rock bottom
And believe they can't go on
They think they have nothing to live for
But I'm here to tell them that there wrong.

There's always an alternative
There's always something you can do
No-one said life would be easy
But never give up on you.

Talk your problems over
With an organisation or a friend
Don't be bullied by another
Don't let them drive you to your end.

The greatest gift of all is life
You have so much more to live
You are stronger than you think
And have so much love to give.

You can turn your darkness into light
You can make it if you try
But it's time for you to choose
It's time for you to live your life, not die.

Written by Elaine Gibbons. ©

MOTHER

You're my Mother
You're my friend
You've been there when I've needed you
And hopefully will be, till the end.

You're my Mother
Who has been patient with me
Not been my judge when I've made a mistake
But has loved me unconditionally.

You're my Mother
Who has taught me right from wrong
When I've been tested by trials
You've been there to guide me along.

You're my Mother and I love you
So these words are sent to say
I wish you a very, very special
And Happy Mothers Day.

Everyday is Mothers Day.

Written by Elaine Gibbons. ©

JUST LOOKING BACK-2013

A lot of things have happened
So many things took place
As I try and recall them
I have a smile upon my face.

January was scary
My job was on the line
The month of June was special
I celebrated with a friend of mine.

The next few months were amazing
I put pen to paper more
Black History month was a celebration
That night for me was an open door.

I've been encouraged by so many
But Mr Noble stands out for me
He gave me so many great ideas
I am so much more that I thought I could be.

I am big and I'm bold
I am 'A Poem on the Wall'
As the year draws to a close
With more confidence I stand tall.

Confident that I can be positive
And do all I hope to achieve
2014 will be a better year
In that I do believe.

As one door closes another will open
A disappointment can be a blessing in disguise
But everything happens for a reason
I won't just stand, I promise to rise.

Written by Elaine Gibbons. ©

CHAPTER THREE- IT'S GOSPEL

"Listen to yourself and in that quietude
you might hear from God."
Maya Angelou

I'VE BEEN SAVED

Please God guide me
And teach me your way
Help me to be obedient
So I don't have to go astray.

Please God give me courage
So I can do your will
And give me daily strength
At times when I need to be still.

Please God help me to do what's right
So that I can be a blessing too
So that I can love and encourage others
To stand and follow you.

Thank you God for protecting me
And keeping me safe from harm
When my enemies try and put me down
I'll always remember to read a Psalm.

Thank you God for your words of wisdom
I use my bible as my guide
To teach me how to walk with Jesus
And in his spirit to abide.

Thank you God
For all you've done for me
For your forgiveness and understanding
But above all, your mercy.

Written by Elaine Gibbons. ©

HIS GRACE AND MERCY

I woke up this morning and gave God thanks
For allowing me to see another day
I know today wasn't promised to me
He could have taken my breath away.

I woke up this morning and gave God thanks
For the health and strength that I need
I can't rely on myself anymore
So with my thanks I sow a good seed.

I woke up this morning and gave God thanks
And asked him to guide and protect me
I don't know the dangers or obstacles
That in my way could always be.

I woke up this morning and gave God thanks
For all blessings that I receive
My job, my home and family
For his love, grace and mercy.

I will always thank God in the morning
And remember to praise him at night
But if I don't live to see tomorrow
Today I've lived it right.

Written by Elaine Gibbons. ©

HE WHO HAS BEEN GOOD TO ME

He makes me smile in the morning
And gives me something to live for
He is attentive to my needs
And is always willing to give much more.

His love is overwhelming
He promised it will never end
He makes my life so much easier
And on him I can depend.

He listens silently to my conversations
And answers when I call
He's there in good and bad times
And there to catch me when I fall.

I try my best to please him
I respect and honour him to
I love him like no other
For him there is nothing I wouldn't do.

I've promised to be faithful
To the one who strengthens me
To the one who gives me courage
And has a hold of my destiny.

So who is he that has been good to me?
He is the one that will love me to the end
He is the one that I can always call upon
He is Jesus my precious friend.

Written by Elaine Gibbons. ©

MY LIFELONG JOURNEY

I know when it began
But can't say when it's to end
Because Jesus is the answer
And on him I must depend.

He opened my eyes
To a world I never knew
He gave me hope
He only chooses a few.

He say's he'll always love me
Until my day is done
He say's he'll never leave me
For me he sacrificed his son.

He changed my heart
He renewed my mind
He has become my everything
A better friend I'll never find.

He's never failed me
This friend of mine
His love is everlasting
Even when I, step out of line.

Peace, love and joy
Is what I've found on my journey
I'm wonderfully blessed
And no-one can take this from me.

I've been a part of his plan
Before being wonderfully made
And as long as I have confidence in him
I don't have to be afraid.

So my journey continues
With me learning everyday
To put my trust in Jesus
Knowing that he will guide me along the way.

Written by Elaine Gibbons. ©

I'M BLESSED

When I wake up in the morning
I'm blessed
When I go to bed at night
I'm blessed.

A home, a job, a car
I'm blessed
Health and strength so far
I'm blessed.

Friends and family that love me
I'm blessed
A little money in my pocket
I'm blessed.

My sight, my hearing and movement
I'm blessed
I don't have to depend upon others
I'm blessed.

I have a peace of mind
I'm blessed
I feel happy to be alive
I'm blessed.

I have so much love to give
I am blessed
I have my life to live
I am blessed.

I have God in my life
I am so blessed
I have so much to give him thanks for
I have no time to be stressed.

Written by Elaine Gibbons. ©

CHAPTER FOUR – LOVE

"It has been said that we need just three things in life, something to do, something to look forward to and someone to love."
Maya Angelou

REAL LOVE

Where do I start?
What do I first describe?
How do I begin to tell you?
How you make me feel inside.

At first it was so ironic
But now it's just so much more
It really is overwhelming
I've found what I was looking for.

I'm happy, I'm ecstatic
I feel I'm living the dream
It's better than I imagined
Let me pause......before I scream.

We share something very special
And not something I've felt before
The love you give is unconditional
And what I feel is so much more.

When we're apart my thoughts are with you
When were together I'm living the dream
Can this feeling really last a lifetime
Can it be as perfect as it seems.

I just wanted to share with you
My thoughts for today
And just to reassure you
That I'm not leaving you, no way.

What I feel comes from deep down inside
The pages are wet because I just cried
Only for joy and not for sorrow
I love you today, and will tomorrow

Written by Elaine Gibbons. ©

WHY (I LOVE YOU)

Because I didn't want to
And I didn't think I would
And even though you told me
I didn't think I should. (Love you)

Because I just thought of us as friends
I wasn't looking for anything more
And even though I'd seen you over the years
You were just someone to adore.

Because you make me feel special
As if you only have eyes for me
You've included me in your life
And that's a wonderful place to be.

Because you treat me like a lady
And you show me much respect
I am cared for, thought of and loved
And none of this did I expect.

Because I've never met anyone like you
No-one's made me feel this way
So I hope this answers your question
As to why with you, I stay.

Written by Elaine Gibbons. ©

BE MINE

I want to blow your mind
With love and affection
I want to keep you sweet
With my full attention.

I want to take you places
You've never been before
I want to make you mine
Because you're the one I adore.

I want to be the one
To hold you real close
I want to whisper in your ear
How much I love you the most.

I want to be there for you
From morning till night
And if you woke up crying
I'd be there to hold you tight.

I want to be there for you
When the sun goes down
I want to be there for you
Even when there are others around.

I want to be your one and only
So please tell me I can
Please give me your heart
And let me be, your woman.

Written by Elaine Gibbons. ©

WE ALL WANT TO BE LOVED

Love is more than a word
It's more than a red rose
It's more than a kiss
Or the day you proposed.

Love is more than a word
It's more than those tears
It's more than those gifts
But it's not to be feared.

Love is more than that house
And it's more than the baby
Love, is loving you
When you ain't got nobody.

Love is, loving you
Because you know you're worth loving
Love is, loving others
By sharing and giving.

Love is letting go
Because love is free
To go where it will
Or, to come back to me.

Love is peace and joy within
It's patient, kind and ever giving
It's the sun, the moon and the stars
It's not just yours but it's also ours.

Love yourself
As God loves you to
It's easy to love yourself
Because loves within you.

Written by Elaine Gibbons. ©

THIS WAS US

Watching a movie with you
Curled up on the sofa
Taking long walks in the park
Making each other laugh, over and over... (I miss this)

Talking over breakfast
And meeting you for lunch
Staring into your eyes over dinner
I really miss that so much.

Setting the shower
Or running the bath
We would get ready to go out
I would call you my better half... (I miss this)

Waiting for you to come home
I'd check my make-up one last time
Everything was in order
Everything was just fine.

Laying in your arms at night
And waking next to you in the morning
Watching your chest rise as you sleep
I didn't even mind that you were snoring.... (I miss
this)

Many conversations we shared
I now miss your company
The precious moments we had
Sometimes I feel so lonely.

I smile at your memory
We shared many years of bliss
And whenever of think of you
I really miss this....(I miss you)

Written by Elaine Gibbons. ©

IT'S FREE

Love is not anger
Love is not hurt
Love is not fatal
It's really nothing of the sort.

Love is not to make you cry
And it's not to see you in pain
Love is a wonderful feeling
And has no motive or gain.

True love is free
There is no price to pay
It should be unconditional
And shouldn't change from yesterday.

If you love me today
Then you should still tomorrow
If you tell me you don't
That may leave me in sorrow.

I can't make you love me
And I can't make you stay
If you want to leave me
Then just walk away.

Let love go…
If it's ready to leave
It will come back to you one day
Of that you must believe, be ready to receive.

Written by Elaine Gibbons. ©

SIMPLY THE BEST

I love you Mother
For the kindness you've shown
For all your hard work
And the way that I've been grown.

You taught me everything I know
With love and affection
Being patient and caring
You steered me in the right direction.

I just want you to know
How much I appreciate you
And will always be grateful
For all the things you still do.

So enjoy this day
My wonderful Mother
You are simply the best
And I will love you forever.

Written by Elaine Gibbons. ©

I PROMISE

I make my vows to you
I make my vows forever
Your love is overwhelming
I pray we'll always be together.

I saw your smile
I felt your kiss
As I held your hand
This was my first wish.

That we'd be standing here together
On this wonderful day
I'd be declaring all my love
In the best possible way.

I promise to meet your needs
And always take care of you
I promise to show honour and respect
In everything I do.

I promise to keep no secrets
And put no other before your love
I'll make sure you feel protected
You're my angel, you're my love.

I promise to be your best friend
You'll be the only one for me
We two will become one
For all the world to see.

All my love, to my love.

Written by Elaine Gibbons. ©

CHAPTER FIVE – MEMORIES

"Blessed are they that mourn, for they
will be comforted"
Mathew 5v4

SAYING GOOD-BYE TO DAD

I held his hand for hours
The night before he died
I told him how much I loved him
Just before my last tear dried.

He squeezed my hand
As the disease spread thru his body
I'll never forget the look in his eyes
As death drew near my daddy.

He was very weary from his fight
He just wanted to be at rest
To be in that better place
Where Jesus only takes the best.

You were the best dad I could ever have
I'm so very proud of you
And even though I said good-bye
I was still in shock without a clue.

Oh dad, oh how I miss you
But can still see your smiling face
I know you're with God's angels
In your final resting place.

He gave me love and encouragement
My memories could last all day
Life took away someone special
But this is what I have to say.

Thank you Dad for all you gave me
For all your love and positivity.
I will love you forever, it will never fade
And I hope to see you again, because of the vow that I
made.

R.I.P.

Written by Elaine Gibbons. ©

MY NEIGHBOUR MY FRIEND

We grew up together
Danny was a great guy
I've just had news of his passing
What else to do but cry.

I'll miss his smile
His charm as well
The pain I feel
No-one can tell.

I can only imagine
The pain you all feel
Of losing a loved one
It may not even seem real.

But Danny's at rest now
And is no more in pain
I hope happy memories soothe you
As you recall them again, and again.

With deepest sympathy
R.I.P DW

Written by Elaine Gibbons. ©

LOVING MEMORIES

No more sadness
No more tears
We were happy to have you in our lives
For so many, many years.

No more sadness
You're in no more pain
You lived your life to the full
But you did not live it in vain.

But now you're gone
We're left to grieve
You've gone home to the Lord
In that we do believe.

You made so many people happy
You made so many of us smile
Always willing to help others
You'd even go that extra mile.

So we say good-bye to the one we love
But hold our memories very dear
We promise never to forget you
As we shed another tear.

Written by Elaine Gibbons. ©

NOT FORGOTTEN

You're gone you've left us
So we sit here and cry
No time to make arrangements
We didn't know you were going to die.

Your death was very sudden
No time to say good-bye
No time to say, we love you
We moan, we grieve, and we sigh.

Farewell our loved one
We laughed, we cried
But we couldn't hold onto you
Not even when we tried.

We'll miss you more than words can tell
We'll always think of you
And we'll smile when we remember
All the things you use to do.

Written by Elaine Gibbons. ©

MISSING YOU

I miss you now
And always will
You'll never be forgotten
I love you still.

Sadness fills my heart
You've been taken away from me
A part of me died with you
Whole again I'll never be.

We spoke about the future
We made plans for months ahead
We didn't know it would end like this
So some things were never said.

I really wish we could've had the time
To say the things we meant
I really wish we could've had the time
More of it together we could have spent.

No more time, now I must say good-bye
No more time to wonder why
Why you were taken away from me
Because you're with the angels
That's where you're suppose to be.

Written by Elaine Gibbons. ©

TWO YEARS LATER...

I miss him so much
I miss his smile
I wish I could see him again
Just for a little while.

Over forty years we spent together
My heart aches everyday
It's been two years I miss him still
When will this pain go away?

He was full of life
You just had to talk to him to tell
A man of honour and good character
He had great principles as well.

No-one tells you about grieving pain
And how hard it's going to be
It's a pain felt like no other
I still don't believe it's happened to me.

Even though time has passed
The pain is still felt deep
I think of him and smile
And sometimes cry myself to sleep.

My Dad was a great man
So loving and kind
Another husband, father or grandfather
My family and I, will never find.

R.I.P Dad.(8.3.2011)

Written by Elaine Gibbons. ©

REST IN PEACE

We miss you……….. (name)
Not even words can tell
But in our hearts
You will always dwell.

We had many years of happiness
A loving relationship too
We never thought that you would have to leave
So now what do we do?

The time has now come
And I must lay you to rest
To be at peace with the angels
Up in heaven with the best.

So rest in peace ………… (name)
It's time to say good-bye
We promise never to forget you
But as we grieve, we know we'll still cry.

Written by Elaine Gibbons. ©

SAYING GOOD-BYE TO YOU

I never thought we'd part
I thought we'd be together forever
I never thought I'd have to say good-bye
Or feel this way, no never.

You've left so many loved ones behind
Our hearts are broken in two
You left so many things unsaid
Oh how we really miss you.

We miss you more than words can tell
Now your time on earth has passed
Flowers will die, memories will fade
But our love for you will always last.

Written by Elaine Gibbons. ©

THINKING OF YOU

Gone but not forgotten
That's how we think of you
You'll always have a place in our hearts
And in our memories too.

You're missed by so many
And loved by them all too
We hope you'll always know
How much we all loved you.

Now we bid you farewell
As you enter your resting place
We promise never to forget you
Or that smile upon your face.

Written by Elaine Gibbons. ©

IT WAS TIME

Your life was cut short
In the midst of your prime
We never wanted you to go
But God said it was time.

Oh how we love you
And miss you more
You will never be forgotten
And that's for sure.

Brothers, sisters, uncles and aunts
The children, neighbours and friends
Your parents and all the others
The list goes on it never ends.

All the lives you touched in love
Are here to say farewell
We hope one day to meet again
But only, time will tell.

So rest in peace the one we love
For we must now all part
We will cherish you memory forever
And hold it in our hearts.

Written by Elaine Gibbons. ©

FOND MEMORIES

You were so beautiful
With a heart of gold
We shared so many memories
We have stories untold.

You were so elegant and stylish
We were so proud of you
You would stand out in a crowd
No matter what you'd do.

You were confident and capable
Of putting others at ease
This was just a part of your nature
You were always ready to please.

You are spoken of so fondly
And remembered just as well
We don't know how we'll cope without you
And of the pain we cannot tell.

So rest in peace my darling
For your life has come to an end
You're gone but not forgotten
But with the angels you descend.

Written by Elaine Gibbons. ©

SOMEONE SO SPECIAL

I've lost someone special
That's left a pain in my heart
I never thought I would envisage
The day when we would ever part.

I've lost someone special
No-one will ever take your place
We'll never talk again
I'll never see your smiling face.

I've lost someone special
A friend to talk to everyday
We use to share those special moments
But now life's taken you away.

I've lost someone special
Whose memory will linger on
My love for you will never cease
Even now that you are gone.

Written by Elaine Gibbons. ©

A DEAR FRIEND

I'll remember you always
Your love will never end
I'll always have fond memories
Of a very dear friend.

You were always there
When I needed you
A kind word, a nice gesture
This would always get me through.

You would never complain
But showed love to one and all
It was you I would depend on
The friend that I would always call.

I'll remember you always
As I lay you to rest
I now feel rest assured
Because God only takes the best.

Written by Elaine Gibbons. ©

HOW TO CONTACT THE AUTHOR

Contact Elaine Gibbons via email
egauthor@aol.co.uk

www.facebook.com/elaine.gibbons

Feel free to contact me for book orders or events. I also frame poems and poster them in up to size A3.

My first book, A Poets Dream ©2010 can also be ordered from me by email or purchased on Amazon.

May I take this opportunity to thank you again for your support.